the Sunday Learning Series presents:
YOU CAN DO CARTOON VOICES, TOO

by *cartoon voice expert* Sunday Muse

illustrations by Tom Kurzanski
additional illustration by John Banks & Keith Eager

For audio materials and script samples visit: bonus.greatbigvoices.com.

The Sunday Learning Series presents: "You Can DO Cartoon Voices, Too"
Copyright © 2009 by Sunday Muse.
www.sundaymuse.com, www.greatbigvoices.com

All rights reserved. No part of this book may be reproduced or transmitted in any form or by any means, electronic or mechanical, including photocopying, recording, or by any information storage and retrieval system, without the written permission of the author, except where permitted by law.

Cover and interior illustrations by Tom Kurzanski, except where otherwise indicated

Book design by Tom Kurzanski

Photography by Graham Powell, except pages 34, 36, 42

CD Voice Talent provided by Shemar Charles, Mark Ramsay, Zoe Kime,
Andrea Camhi, Liam Tully, Juliana Badovinac.
Recorded at Clare Burt Recording Studios

Chapter Four "Mystical Forest" illustrated by John Banks

Chapter Four "Sally & Charlie" illustrated by Keith Eager

Wonder Buddies, Super Baby Bea, Chronicles of the Forest, and *The Slave Pharaoh* script excerpts written by Andrew Sabiston, WGC

Cogg, The Time Benders, and *Brain Storm & Me* script excerpts written by Gareth Bennett

This book is dedicated to my mentor and friend, Alan Bleviss.

Forward
by Jessie Thomson

I first met Sunday Muse about 10 years ago when she auditioned for an animated TV series that I was casting called "Rolie Polie Olie." What impressed me the most about Sunday besides her undeniable talent as a performer was her "process" of creating a character. Sunday never just jumps in to another character's voice; she always seems to mix the palette of her many voice creations and colors in a more organic way. Her imagination is always engaged fully. What develops is a character voice that is unique, never derivative and always "pure Sunday"!

Sunday has always been interested in teaching kids. They are generally more open-minded than adults in my opinion. It's just one of the reasons I too enjoy working with kids. It seems a perfect fit. Sunday Muse teaching voice character development for cartoons to child actors! Then she told me that she had written this book. I was amazed and impressed.

When I read this book, I was so blown away by how imaginative and fun it is, kind of like Sunday! I'm not suggesting that it isn't a practical guide to the world of animation for kids and their parents, because it most certainly is that, but with a whole section dedicated to the "biz."

What this book offers is a great balance between "the creative process" and the "practical" sides of the business of cartoons. I've always felt that "creative" and "business" is a challenging marriage, but Sunday has managed to present both sides of the business with great clarity and most importantly a great sense of fun. As I have always believed about cartoon performing "If it ain't fun, something's wrong."

I highly recommend this book to all actors, kids and parents of kids who are interested in a career in cartoon voice acting. It is an essential tool. And it's a lot of fun!

~~*Jessie Thomson*
Casting & Voice Director for animated series:
Franklin, Miss Spider, Babar, Atomic Betty,
Care Bears, Jane & the Dragon, Rolie Polie Olie.

TABLE of CONTENTS

I. INTRODUCTION
   THE SUNDAY MUSE STORY 09

II. CHAPTER ONE
   WARM UP: WAKE UP THE OL' VOICEBOX! 16

III. CHAPTER TWO
   THE BEGINNING: HOW TO MAKE YOUR VOICE A CARTOON VOICE 17

IV. CHAPTER THREE
   CHOOSE A "CARTOONY" CHARACTER 21

V. CHAPTER FOUR
   TAKE THE CARTOON JOURNEY: CREATE YOUR OWN STORY OR SCRIPT 30

VI. CHAPTER FIVE
   ROLE PLAY: PLAY WITH SOME SCRIPTS 33

VII. CHAPTER SIX
   THINK LIKE A PROFESSIONAL: "TWO IMPORTANT ROOMS AND ONE IMPORTANT GUY." 35

VIII. CHAPTER SEVEN
   PRACTICE, PRACTICE, PRACTICE: PUT TO USE WHAT YOU HAVE LEARNED 49

IX. CHAPTER EIGHT (FOR PARENTS)
   HOW THE CARTOON VOICES YOU HEAR MAKE CARTOON VOICES A CAREER 50

X. APPENDIX
   BIOGRAPHY & THANKS 61

Introduction: The Sunday Muse Story

My name is Sunday Muse ... yes, for *real*. I was born on a Sunday and my parents were hippies. We were 100 percent vegan and, at that time, I was the *only* girl in my school with long blonde hair that ate almond butter and alfalfa sprout sandwiches.

I was terribly embarrassed by it all, and felt like an "**ODDBALL**" in a world full of "normal" children who said and did normal things with their normal families. I was an only child who liked seeing the world as make believe: trees had faces, kettles had smiles, shoes had mouths, scratches on walls looked like little people, cars had different personalities and toes had something to say about any situation I found myself in.

I searched constantly for those little talking characters in the background I saw in my world and that nobody else seemed to see. Or so I *thought*. These things gave me a sense that there were always little people or objects around to keep me company.

I created voices for these "**characters**" and entertained my friends and family with them. The car with a voice, the leg that talked, the look on my mom's face in the mornings. *Everything* had a voice. Even my **BAD** days had a voice. My **SAD** days, my **SCARED** days, my **HAPPY** days, my *quiet* days. All my days had special and different voices.

The world of make believe is like a cartoon. Anything can happen ... anything can come to life and speak. So many things in life that I observed or that I found funny, left me with a desire to see more. My imaginary world as a child became my own cartoon land,

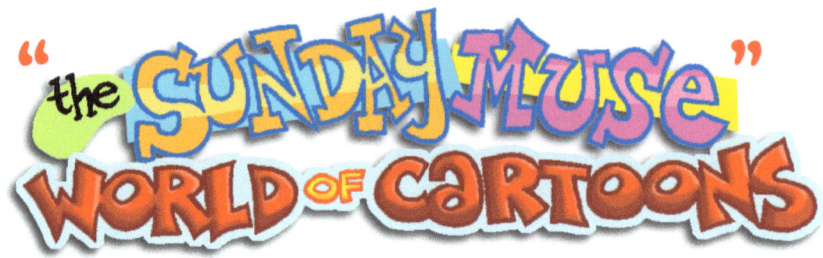

For me, everything in life has a voice in cartoons.

Now, I have a question for you:
Do you think you could try and see your world this way – just for fun?
See what your baby toe has to say, *bonjour!* or the voice your pillow makes when he "talks" to you? *mornin' sunshine!* Think about the time you bonked your head on something. Could you make a sound effect for that experience?

If you were to write it out, what would the words look like? Think about it like this:

Here's my funny word for _____ : _____
                                real word   funny word

Here's one for _____ : _____
                   real word   funny word

Introduction: the Sunday Muse Story

WHY DO I LIKE DOING CARTOON VOICES FOR A LIVING?

My job is very *freeing*! I get to really be **ME**. I assume most of you have seen cartoons, but if you haven't, picture a colorful character from a book your mom or dad reads to or with you. Think of a book you might enjoy reading on your own.

That's what a cartoon looks like! A cartoon is an *exaggerated* version of us. Becoming a cartoon requires that we **EXPAND** ourselves and get a lot **BIGGER** in our facial expressions and body movements.

YOUR cartoon is an exaggerated version of **YOU**! Or it could be an exaggerated version of me, or of anyone. Have you seen caricatures? You know those little drawings that people sketch at fairs and festivals? They look like an exaggerated version of the people the artists are drawing.

To exaggerate **YOU**, your voice has to get **MUCH LOUDER**, and your hands need to move when you speak. I grew up Italian, and if you know Italians, they express a lot with their hands to emphasize what they say. This is really important when doing cartoon voices. You need to stand in front of a microphone, get louder, and **MOVE** your hands - like when you play charades - and **ANIMATE** your body and your voice!

Introduction: the Sunday Muse Story

When I was young, I spent a lot of time with my Italian grandmother, which is "**NONNA**" in Italian. She didn't speak a word of English, so it was a little challenging to communicate with her. I would hang out in the bathroom, in front of the mirror, make faces and make up characters all day to keep myself entertained. I did this for hours! *Why?* I don't know, I think it was because I was so expressive as a kid, and I needed a creative outlet ... **badly.**

So many things made me laugh. *HAHAhahaha* The one thing I discovered when I was looking in the mirror, making faces, was that when you make a face, you **change,** and your voice starts to change.

I learned that if I go like this   or maybe I go like this ...

I might start talking with a funny voice. By playing with my face in the mirror – making funny faces – and playing with all different emotions, like **ANGER** and *joy*, I discovered that I had a whole *repertoire* of characters, all these people that I could make voices for or "**VOICE**." I learned to do something I loved! It was at that point, that I started to entertain people with my talents.

SHHHHHHHHHH

A little secret...

I still get **SCARED** before I try out a voice in front of people, because I fear that I might look or sound too silly, make a fool of myself or be laughed at, but once I jump in, I feel so full of **ENERGY** and **JOY** that I just want to keep going. I'd like to encourage you to do the same. Take risks while reading this book! Use your voice in ways you might never have imagined. Open yourself to that wonderful, magical, wacky world of **cartoons**. Have fun! You can **NEVER** be too silly when trying out or trying on a voice.

For those of you who don't know, I do cartoon voices for a living, and I teach children of all ages all over the world how to do them. I love being able to pass on all the tools that took me **YEARS** to learn.

Do you know Cheer Bear from the *Care Bears* movies? That's me! I also play Baby Binky on *Rolie Polie Olie*, Freddi in *Time Warp Trio*, Pepper in *Jane and the Dragon*, Gibby from *The Wumblers*, Lara in *Willa's Wildlife*, George's puppet Wally from *Arthur*, and many more voices you might recognize from popular cartoon shows and movies! I couldn't ask for a better job, and I am grateful.

Introduction: the Sunday Muse Story

Okay, let's get started-- **WAIT**!
I almost forgot, I can't believe it.
First, I'd like to introduce you to six **GREAT KIDS**. You can call them the
"**CARTOON GANG**."

SHEMAR JULIANA MARK

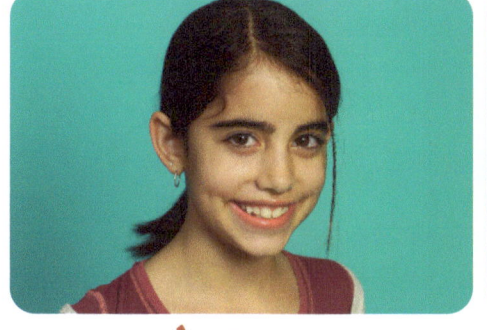ANDREA 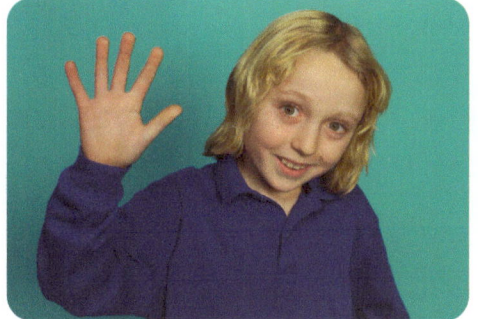LIAM 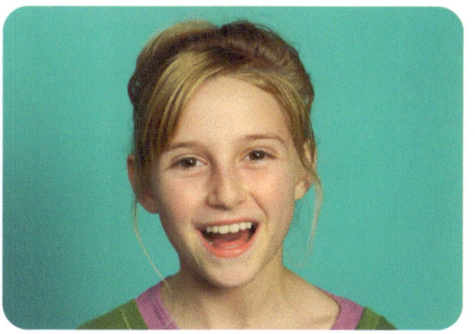ZOE

I selected these kids to be a part of this book so you can **SEE** and **HEAR** how cartoons are done! They are my helpers. Say hello to the gang.

⭐ **INSTRUCTION:** Listen to **TRACK ONE** for Sunday's Intro plus a few of her cartoon voices.*

Hello, Gang!

*download the tracks at bonus.greatbigvoices.com

Chapter 1
Warm Up: Wake Up the Ol' Voicebox!

For a warm up, we're gonna need some good rap music.

Yuppers. You will hear Rap with no lyrics, just background music! As part of the warm up, you will make up your own **RAP** on the spot. I think this is an important thing to do.

WHY?

So we can **LET GO** of our fears, and have **FUN** and be **GOOFY**. Cartoons are goofy too, remember. The purpose of this is to have fun, **PROJECT** your voice, really do it up **BIG** and 'not think.'

(Just say things off the top of your head to the rhythm of the rap.)

Let me start you off with an example of Shemar and Juliana doing a Rap. Then, just like Shemar and Juliana, you can give yourself topics and see what comes out of your mouth without thinking. Just let whatever comes out, come out, and have fun!

⭐ **INSTRUCTION:** Play **TRACK TWO**, for Shemar's Rap. Play **TRACK THREE** for Juliana's Rap. Play **TRACK FOUR** for Rap without lyrics.

Introduction: the Sunday Muse Story

Chapter 2
The Beginning: How to Make YOUR Voice a CARTOON Voice

To begin, we need to break down the difference between our normal speaking voice and our cartoon voice. We call this "normal talking" and "CARTOON TALKING."

Normal talking is how you speak to your friends and family every day. Cartoon talking is *much more* **exaggerated**, ANIMATED and requires that you express yourself in the **BIGGEST** way possible. For example, when you are doing a voice for a cartoon and your cartoon character is supposed to feel **ANGRY**, you need to express that anger

like a **GIANT** anger, A **LION'S** anger, **ELEPHANT** anger,

or just think of anything that is *WAY* bigger than you are in real life.

You may look silly, but it will gear you up to deliver your **CARTOON** voice.

You never want to go "small" with your voice.

⭐ **INSTRUCTION:** Play **TRACKS FIVE** through **EIGHT** to hear the difference between *normal* energy and *cartoon* energy!

Come on Jake, we have to go, or we'll be late for the party.

(NORMAL- FIVE & SEVEN, CARTOON- SIX & EIGHT)

One: PROJECTION

We *MUST* get **LOUDER** to do cartoon voices. Don't forget that our voices have to go all way from the recording studio, onto the television screen and pop out of the cartoon character's mouth. That's a long way to travel. If we don't speak our words with **PROJECTION** and *clarity*, they end up sounding strange. No one will be able to hear them.

Listen to a cartoon with your eyes closed for **FIVE** (5) minutes. Do you hear how **BIG** the voices sound? Now, try projecting your own voice as **LARGE** and **LOUD** as you are able.

Two: USE YOUR BODY

Have you ever been so **EXCITED** when sharing a story with your friends about something cool that happened to you? What does your body do when you are telling your story?

Do you use your 👐 hands 👐?
Do you jump **up** and **down**?
Do you **MOVE AROUND** a lot?

Probably. That's the same thing that you do when doing your cartoon voice.

Use your hands and arms to *express* yourself. Just like when we play charades, we have to **MOVE** our arms a lot to get our point across, to get people to understand that we are giving the clues to the right answer. With cartoons, we move our arms while speaking, which gives our voice **ENERGY**. If you've ever seen Jim Carrey doing a voice for a cartoon, he **NEVER** sits or stands still! He's **ALWAYS** moving his arms and face like a **DING DONG** to express himself in the cartoon character he's playing. The result? His voices are fantastic!

The Beginning: How to Make YOUR Voice a CARTOON Voice

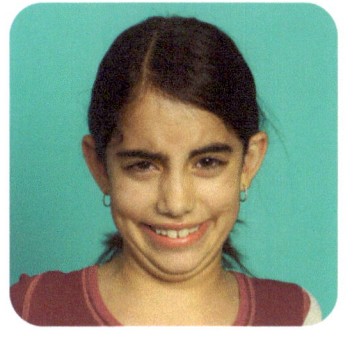

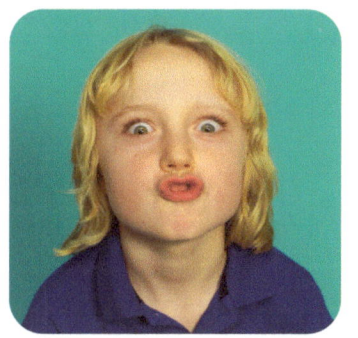

Three: USE YOUR FACE

Just like it is important to use your body, you also need to use your face to make your cartoon voice come to life. Think again about telling your exciting story to friends. Do you just use a **LOW** voice and keep your face **STRAIGHT**, or do you *raise* your eyebrows, open your eyes **WIDE**, open your mouth **WIDER**, **PUFF UP** your cheeks, or do something else to show how you feel about the story? When creating a cartoon voice, you do the same. Raise your eyebrows, smile big, squint your eyes. Every change in facial expression brings new and bigger energy to the voice.

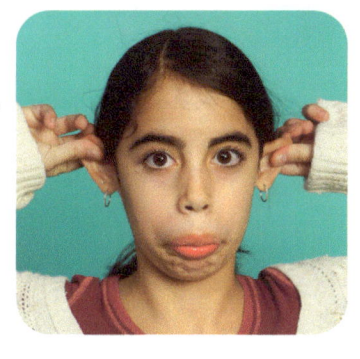

TRY IT! Make a silly face and project your voice as you say something. Say anything. Say, **"I'm tired of playing. I wanna go home."** Say it in your normal voice, and then say it in your cartoon voice. Do you hear and feel the difference?

Now you understand the difference between "real" life and "**CARTOON**" life.

The simple fact is this: Cartoons are a whole lot

BIGGER.

Cartoons are also very **SILLY**.

If you're going to do cartoons, you need to be silly, too!

Chapter 3
Choose a "Cartoony" Character

Okay, so let's take the plunge and really dig **DEEP** into the cartoon world. This part is really cool, because you can now choose a **CHARACTER** from the next page and explore similar cartoon types that you see on television every day.

Get ready to "try on the character," imagine stepping into his/her life and out of your own, then *imitate* the character and finally **BECOME** the **CARTOON**. Yesssss! I'll walk you through the steps.

FIRST, CHOOSE A CHARACTER YOU'D LIKE TO BE.
(flip to the next page)

Once you have chosen a character, take a look at the way he/she is standing, what the arms are doing, the legs, the *posture*, the *facial expressions* and **MOOD** of the character. Is he/she happy, nervous, angry, shy?

Now, **IMITATE** the character. Use your bathroom or bedroom mirror, so you can watch yourself as you transform into the character. Imagine you are peeling off the mask of your character; now, paste it on your face. Imagine you are wearing a **MASK**. Make your character's expressions super **GIANT** on your own face.

You Can DO Cartoon Voices, Too

Choose a "Cartoony" Character

Now you are ready to enter into the **LIFE** of the cartoon character you chose, and **YOU** are going to create it with your own **IMAGINATION**.

HOW?

Ask yourself questions about the character:

• **WHERE** do you think the character is located? Is it the *beach, kitchen, sky, ocean, park* or *dining room*? Be sure to choose the location.

• **WHAT** is the **ACTION** of the character? Think active verbs. Is the character *pushing, pulling, luring, climbing, walking, standing, jumping up and down* or *flying a kite*?

• **WHAT** is the character **FEELING**? Is he/she *happy, mad, sad, glad, jealous, anxious, frustrated*? You choose. You have felt all of these emotions in your life, so you know what they feel like and you know how you expressed them with your body and your face. You know from the inside out. Now, you get to give these emotions life inside your character.

• **WHO** do you imagine the character is talking to? Is it a *cousin, stranger, the dog, him/herself* or *whom*? Why I want you to think about this is because, just like in real life, the way we talk to our dog is far different from the way we might talk to a stranger or our mother.

> **NOTE**
> Give yourself a few minutes to make up your mind.
> REMEMBER THIS IS FROM YOUR IMAGINATION, SO DON'T WORRY ABOUT MAKING THE "PERFECT" CHOICE. THERE IS NO RIGHT ANSWER.

Choose a "Cartoony" Character

Here's an Example:
Shemar's character is "Wes the Cowboy"

- WES IS IN THE WILD WEST. (this is the location)
- HE IS FEELING ANGRY (this is the emotion)
- HE IS FIGHTING (this is the action)

What is the first thing Shemar has to do? Since he is angry, if you were doing his voice, you would express **ANGER** in his body in as big of a way possible.

Then you would have to express how he might be **FIGHTING** in as big of a way possible.

Now you would PROJECT YOUR VOICE, speaking in a big way while fighting in the Wild West and showing the emotion he is feeling with your body.

You are now

...the cartoon character!

⭐ **INSTRUCTION:** Play **TRACK NINE** to hear Shemar's example. Play **TRACKS TEN, ELEVEN & TWELVE** for examples of **"THE GANG"** making up characters.

Mark's character is "JOHNNY THE BULLY" He's at the schoolyard (location)

He's frustrated (emotion)　　　　He's teasing a kid (action)　　　　Action/emotion combined

Zoe's character is "*a little girl*" She's in the closet (location)

She's feeling sad and lonely (emotion)　　She's talking to her turtle (action)　　Action/emotion combined

Liam's character is "Super Baby" Super Baby is on a desert Island (location)

He's feeling nervous/excited (emotion)　　He's soaring through the sky (action)　　Action/emotion combined

Choose a "Cartoony" Character

HERE ARE A FEW PICTURES SOME OF "THE GANG" DREW OF THEIR CHARACTERS!

Just like how a *mime* does his work, show me how you express your character's **emotion** in your body, using your face and arms to do it in a **BIG** way. On the count of **3** ... **1**, **2**, **3**!

Now, go **BIGGER** ... **BIGGER** ... **MORE** ... **MORE** ... **MORE** ... *come on you can do it* ... **GOOD**!

Now, show me how you express your **ACTION** in your body. Go **BIGGER**, **MORE**, **MORE**, **MORE**, **MORE**, **MORE** ... **GOOD**!

Let's hear what you have to say from that place. Don't worry about not saying the right thing. Just *try* it. Let your imagination run

GO FOR IT!

HOLY KAMOLEE, *good job!*

A lot of the kids I teach start laughing when they really commit to doing this, which is a **GOOD** sign. It means you are getting into the *fun* of it. Once you've gotten the *giggles* out of you, try it again. Choose *another* character from the previous pages. Taking risks is part of doing cartoon voices. Be willing to look **SILLY**! Like me! even **RIDICULOUS**.

When we watch cartoons, the characters usually **ARE** silly and ridiculous. The actor (**YOU**) behind the voice of the cartoon characters **needs** to act silly, too.
It is a whole lotta fun I tell yah!

I **LOVE** what I do; I love doing **CARTOON VOICES**.

Choose a "Cartoony" Character

You can try **ALL** the characters in this book if you wish, or do one per day for practice. But don't forget the *three most important things* to bring your characters to life:

USE LOTS OF ...

> **TIP**
>
> **Record** yourself while doing the voice of the characters. Use a taperecorder or even a Karaoke machine. Once you've recorded your voice, listen to it. Close your eyes when you do. Ask yourself:
> *"Do I sound like a cartoon?"*
> Be honest. Most times, we need lots and lots of practice to sound like a cartoon. Don't be disappointed or give up if you don't yet sound like a cartoon character. Keep trying. You **CAN** do it!

Introduction: the Sunday Muse Story

This improv exercise is fun to do with your family, friends or alone. On the previous page, there is a picture of a forest that includes two characters, **CHARLIE** and **SALLY**. I encourage you to step into the **CARTOON WORLD** in the picture, and create from your imagination, all the details you see in that world. Try to see everything through your character's eyes. Remember that this is a journey into this forest - so keep the action moving forward with your observations every time you ask the question *"What happens now?"* **ACTION** is what makes a story *EXCITING*.

① Look closely at the forest picture and choose which character you'd like to be: Charlie or Sally.

② Now, figure out the voice you will use. Just for an example, let's say you choose Charlie. What does his voice sound like?

③ Next, look closely at the picture of the forest, and all the little details - are there little creatures? Faces in the trees?

④ In your character's voice, describe 10 things you see. Try and experience it through your character, and pay attention to what you are seeing, feeling and hearing.

⑤ Choose one of the details you found in the picture and ask yourself *"What happens now?"*

Your answers will help you create your story and maybe even your own script!

REMEMBER ... you ARE the character!

Here is an example to help get you started:

WHAT HAPPENS NOW?　　　　　　　　　**WHAT HAPPENS NOW?**

SALLY: I see large footprints.

I am looking for a bear, so we can follow him to the place he hides his honey jars!

WHAT HAPPENS NOW?

CHARLIE: We spot Mr. Bear behind the big tall tree, but he growls at us when we ask him about the honey so we run for our lives!!!

> **NOTE** Creating your cartoon journey might make you **laugh** your **head off**, but don't be afraid to say what you *think*. It's a great idea to **RECORD YOURSELF** and listen to the recording to help you find areas of improvement.

> **TIP** Close your eyes and ask yourself, "*Do I sound like a cartoon?*" Keep in mind: **projection, action in the body, emotion in the body,** and **exaggerate with your face and hands** to **SHOW** what you are feeling. This is how you get connected to what you are saying.

Chapter 5
Role Play: Play With Some Scripts

Dear awesome kids:
I am thrilled that you have come this far! You are amazing.

Just for **YOU**, I have made a few sample **CARTOON SCRIPTS*** available on my website, just like the actors use in the movies and on TV. Notice that there are a few characters on each page from which you can choose to be. Read these **ALOUD** on your own or with a friend, and **PRACTICE** being the cartoon character.

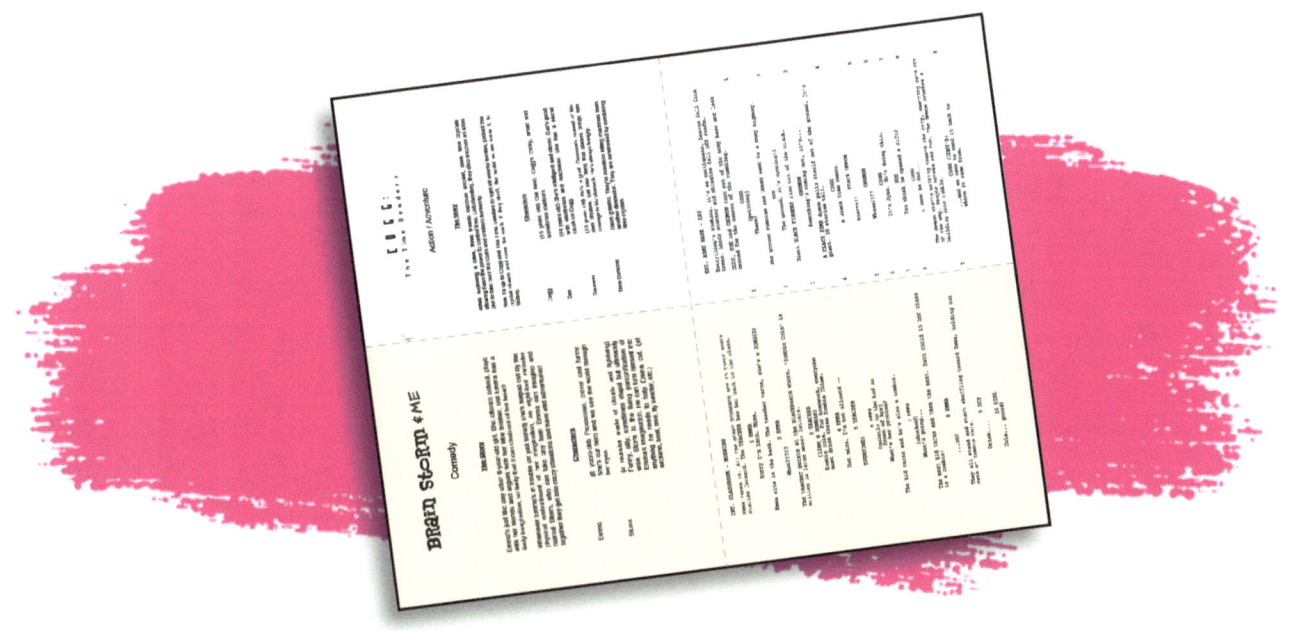

*Download PDF scripts at: bonus.greatbigvoices.com

Now that you have learned some *major* pointers on becoming a cartoon character you can record your scene and ask yourself: "*DO I SOUND LIKE A CARTOON?*"

REMEMBER:

 **PROJECTION,**

 **EXPRESS WITH YOUR ARMS,**

 **EXPRESS WITH YOUR FACE** and

Also, just for fun, how would you draw your character? I will admit, I am not very good at drawing, but I love to see what comes out when I just let my pencil hit the page.

Give it a try!

> **TIP**
>
> When reading a script, notice the **punctuation**. If you see a **comma**, it means *pause*. If you see a **period**, it means *pause*, too, but just *a wee bit longer*. That way, you are reading the script as it is **meant** to be read. If you don't pause, you just have run-on sentences with no breaths in between. It's like when someone is talking to you without taking a breath and without stopping. You can't get a word in edgewise and you lose interest in what the person is saying. Without pauses in the right places, conversation and scripts become boring or overwhelming to the listener. So **pause** when you see the **punctuation** marks! Your teachers will be **proud**.

Chapter 6
Think Like a Professional: "Two Important Rooms & One Important Guy"

I chose these two characters, because they are very important in the world of professional cartoon voice work. Without them, I could not do my job.

MR. CONTROL BOOTH   **MR. SOUND STUDIO**

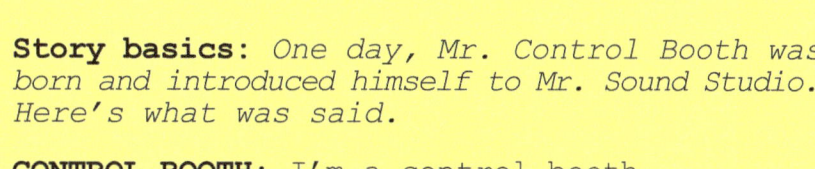

Story basics: *One day, Mr. Control Booth was born and introduced himself to Mr. Sound Studio. Here's what was said.*

CONTROL BOOTH: I'm a control booth.

SOUND STUDIO: And I'm a sound studio.

CONTROL BOOTH: Good for you.

SOUND STUDIO: Good for you, too.

CONTROL BOOTH: I have a whole bunch of knobs to control you. So, there!

SOUND STUDIO: Oh, yeah? Well, I have microphones to talk into and headsets to listen to yourself through, and music stands for scripts, AND you can't do anything with me until I give you sound.

CONTROL BOOTH: Oh, yeah?

SOUND STUDIO: Yeah.

You Can Do Cartoon Voices, Too

Have you ever wondered how the actors who do the voices of your favorite cartoons make a living?

INTRODUCING: A DAY IN THE LIFE OF A VOICE ACTOR

When you first walk into the room where the actors record cartoon voices, you will see that it is divided into two parts:

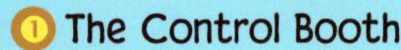

① The Control Booth and **② The Sound Studio**

Why do you think it's called the control booth?

The control booth is where all the control knobs are located on a big board. This is where the technician or engineer sits and adjusts volume, vocal levels and records your voice that will go with the cartoon characters we see on TV or in the movies. The talent of the technician is what makes your voice sound great!

©iStockphoto.com/Mike Bentley

Why is it called a Sound Studio?

The sound studio is an area with microphones, music stands for scripts and headphones. This is where you give voice to your characters and where famous actors in the cartoon movies "do" their voices. The sound room has a door to it. This is designed in a way to keep outside sounds out of the room when you are recording. You want it to be as quiet as possible in this recording room, so it usually has a lot of extra padding in the walls.

Think Like a Professional: "Two Important Rooms and One Important Guy"

Why do we need an ENGINEER?
*(He's ONE Important Guy!
Let's call him Joe.)*

Joe makes you sound good, **sets up** the microphones, headphones and music stands. He also **records** your voice and **edits** (takes out) the things that don't work. He keeps the whole studio running smoothly.

He *might* even make coffee or tea for you.

Hello, Joe.

Thanks, Joe.

How do you get a cartoon voice job, so your voice can be on TV or in the movies?

Before the voice of *Franklin* was chosen for the lovable turtle character we now see on TV, the young boy actor, Noah Reid, had to do an audition. This is how he got the part. Auditions are important. An audition is how I landed the part of *Cheer Bear* in the *Care Bears* movies, and *Pepper* in *Jane and the Dragon*.

Now, how do YOU do it? First things First...

THE AUDITION:

An audition is where you go to "try out" for the part you want to play. It's like an interview for a job, only you read from a scene, so the boss can hear your cartoon voice. You read the scene or copy.

What is copy?

Copy is the scene written on pages that you are given before an audition, also known as "sides." You have time to look it over and prepare. This script is usually two to eight pages in length, depending on the part (character you will be playing). Let's say you are going to audition (also known as 'read for') for "Larry the Bear." You would be given the copy/sides with Larry's scene. The scene includes directions for the action that is going on between characters.

TAKE A LOOK AT THE NEXT PAGE.

Think Like a Professional: "Two Important Rooms and One Important Guy"

EXAMPLE:

EXT. SHOT *Larry the Bear is sitting on a tree stump, slumped over. Chester the Squirrel is trying to cheer him up.*

1 **LARRY** *(line 1)*
Boy, I wish our team didn't lose again.

2 **CHESTER**
We did our best Larry, and winning isn't everything, you know. Think about how hard we practiced before the game and how good we all felt.

3 **LARRY**
Yeah, but what does it matter?

4 **CHESTER**
It matters because we were having fun playing soccer. It was the fun that brought us all together and allowed us to really become a team. I don't know about you, but I made new friends from the team, and that is really special to me.

5 **LARRY**
Hmm. Maybe I am too focused on winning, but I can't help it. My older brother is really competitive with me and is always rubbing it in my face that he won, he won.

6 **CHESTER**
C'mon, Larry. Let's go and get a honey bowl from Mrs. Beeeesly.

BREAKING DOWN COPY

When I read audition copy, I see the script as a *musical score*. A script, like a musical score has different *rhythms*, *NOTES* and *voices* and it also has a beginning, middle and end. I understand that if I read every line the same, it's like singing a song with one note. How *boring* would that be? My job is to vary it up. For those of you who know music, great. For those who don't, that's okay too. I will outline some very basic techniques that anyone can use just like I do.

FOR EXAMPLE:

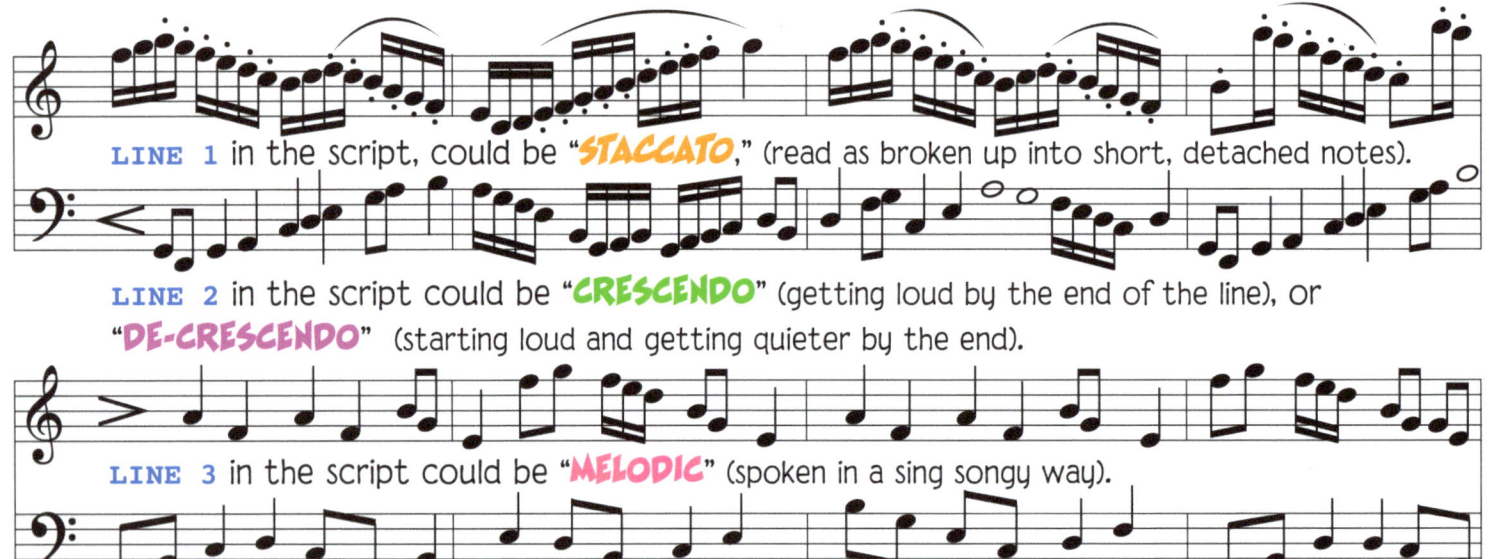

LINE 1 in the script, could be "*STACCATO*," (read as broken up into short, detached notes).

LINE 2 in the script could be "*CRESCENDO*" (getting loud by the end of the line), or "*DE-CRESCENDO*" (starting loud and getting quieter by the end).

LINE 3 in the script could be "*MELODIC*" (spoken in a sing songy way).

INSTRUCTION: Play **TRACK THIRTEEN** for an example of "*7 Different Ways to deliver your lines.*"

RHYTHMS:

When we speak to people, we shift from *fast talking* to **slow talking**; to medium-tempo talking. We're just not aware of it. But if you are in a hurry, you are going to speak **FAST**, and if you are trying to make a point, you might speak **SLOWLY**. When you read your script, you can break down each line you say into fast, slow, or medium tempo. You have total control over which *rhythm* you choose.

Every day, we **FEEL** something, some emotions. We are *happy*, **MAD**, *sad*, **ANNOYED** or whatever, so it is important to give your cartoon character **EMOTIONS** too.

Let's try something.

Choose a **CHARACTER** from one of the scripts in this book and give it a *different emotion* for each line your character has to say in the script (just like you did in the last chapter!)

Now choose a *different action* for each line your character has to say in the script.

WRITE YOUR EMOTION AND ACTION DOWN on your script, *BEFORE* each of your character's lines. Below I give you an example in green to show you what I mean.

SALLY

(happy/ searching) Jake is under the bed, I just know it ...
There you are, Jake!"

At this point, it is important to ask yourself "WHO AM I TALKING TO?" Who is the character that you are playing talking to in the scene? Is it *Lu-Lu the Ladybug* or **BUDD THE SLUG**, **LARRY THE BEAR**, **UNCLE SAM**, Aunt Wendy, **MR. MUFFIN HEAD**, or maybe **JUDY THE JUNK TRUCK**.

YOU decide.

Pretend you are talking to *someone you know* in your real life. Imagine WHO it is. This could be a **person** or an **object**. It's totally up to you. This will make your script reading *stronger*. Give yourself a moment to think to whom you are talking. If you

UNCLE BILL   UNCLE BEAR

are a bug in *Miss Spider* and you are yelling about important stuff to another bug that is your uncle in the script, it's fair for me to ask, "*Have you ever talked to a bug before about important stuff?*" If the answer is yes, use that experience. If not, you're going to have to think a bit about how you might communicate with a bug and what it might be like to BE a bug yourself. I know you kids are so **IMAGINATIVE**, but most often we actors need to *replace* the bug uncle in the script with one of our own uncles or other relatives to create a **true** and **interesting** read.

If the script only includes your character's lines and nothing else, **INVENT** or **MAKE UP** someone to talk to. Think about how you'd deliver the lines in the script to a **friend** or an **aunt** or **uncle**.

Here is an example of a *monologue* (one character speaking, but with no response from any other character). In this example, **BUDD THE SLUG** tries to hurry down the street. That is the **ACTION** of the script (or copy).

> **BUDD THE SLUG**
> Oh no, I'm going to be late for the spring carnival!
> I wish I could move faster. Arggggh ... why couldn't I
> be a super-fast bumblebee with super-duper bumble wings?
> I hope Aunt Spacey McFly doesn't eat all the ice cream.
> She always beats me to it ... Ohhhhh, I'm tired. This
> moving fast just isn't for me.

You might imagine that Budd is talking to his neighbor, Mr. Flaxseed. Perhaps Mr. Flaxseed is a lot like your real life Uncle George, so you could imagine your own uncle when you say the lines.

Does that make sense? I hope so.

TIP — Repeat the **Top Three Pointers** for becoming a cartoon character!
I CANNOT STRESS THESE ENOUGH!
DON'T FORGET TO:

1) **EXAGGERATE the ACTIONS you have chosen.**

2) **EXAGGERATE the EMOTIONS using your arms.**

3) **MOVE YOUR FACE while you speak, and practice reading your script.**

Now I'd like to introduce you to the microphone and go over some techniques that will help you when reading a script.

MICROPHONE TECHNIQUE:

When you are in the sound studio reading your lines, you have to **PROJECT INTO THE MICROPHONE**. Say hello to the microphone and for fun, pretend you are both characters.

Hello, Mr. **Mic**!

(This is pronounced **MIKE**.)

Hey.

Mr. Mic's a *cool* guy, he doesn't say much.

Stand about a foot away from the microphone (the mic) and treat him like he's your friend.

SALUTE THE MIC!

"Hello Mr. Microphone. How are you? That's good. Me too. Okay ... let's do **CARTOON** voices!"

The mic wants you to like him, **BUT** he doesn't want you to get *too* close.

Keep your distance, because the sound becomes DISTORTED if you get too close to Mr. Mic.

POPPING "**P**"s from words like "**PORKY PORKY PENGUINS**" blows the directors and engineers **OUT OF THEIR CHAIRS.** You will hurt their ears if you are too close to the mic.

The microphone is a **STRANGE** object for some people. If you have never been in front of a mic, it might be strange at first, so I'm going to walk you through some basic steps. When the mic is placed in front of you here's what you do: PROJECT (get louder)! You may feel like you are yelling, but you have to be **WAY** louder than in real life to capture the CARTOON in you.

Connect to the *emotion* you have chosen for your first line. Mime it. Go over the top, EXPRESSING it with your whole body. Really *feel* it or else it's fake. It won't feel real to listeners.

MOST people don't know this:

If you go to an audition for a **CARTOON**, you will read *by yourself*. Nobody reads opposite you like they would in **TV**, **FILM** or *theatre* auditions. **YOU** and **YOU** alone read your character's lines, one after the other.

> **TIP** → When saying your lines the first time try them as a **loud whisper**. When we **whisper**, we have to really try to get our point across. Then read it with your cartoon voice and *really try* to get your point across.

Pick your STRESS WORDS. Which words in each sentence would you like to STRESS? UNDERLINE them.

What happens when you go into the audition room?

When you are called into the audition room, a *casting director* will be present. WHO? The casting director guides you through an audition, telling you what to do so that the big boss, **THE PRODUCER**, will hear you deliver a *fantastic* read of your character.

The Casting director is usually very nice, and here are some of the things she might say:

"Hello, Zoe, how are you?"

"Good, thanks."

Think Like a Professional: "Two Important Rooms and One Important Guy"

Casting Director
"Okay, let's get you in the sound studio and set you up."

Joe the engineer will adjust your **microphone** to your height and **headphones** to fit your head. Once you go into the **sound studio**, you will place your script on a **music stand** so you can read it. Then the casting director might ask you if you have any **questions**.

Casting Director
"Do you have any questions, Zoe?"

If you have questions, ask them at this time.

Casting Director
"Okay, Zoe, you can begin your read when you are ready."

And AWAY YOU GO!

After you have finished reading your lines the casting director might get you to do it again with some feedback. She might say, **"Can you try it with more energy?"** or **"Can you read it like you are really happy?"** AWAY YOU GO, doing what she asks.

Sometimes, the casting director won't ask you *anything*. She'll just say, **"Thanks, Zoe, you're done now."** At that point, you can leave the room.

You just did your **FIRST AUDITION**.

Now you get to wait a bit to find out whether you get a *callback* or not.

What's a callback?

When **PRODUCERS** and *casting directors* can't make up their minds on 'WHO' should get the part, they will call you *and* a few other kids back to **re-do** the audition. **Sometimes**, they will send you a *different* part of the script to prepare, so you can put all the **TOOLS** you learned in this book to use *once again*.

I wish you the *best* and have all the **CONFIDENCE** in you, whether you *get* the part *or not*. We must **PERSEVERE** to make **CARTOON VOICES** a career. Nobody said it was *easy*, but if you keep at it, I have no doubt that something **GOOD** will come for you.

Chapter 7
Practice, Practice, Practice: Put to Use What You Have Learned

Well, we have come to the end of our lesson, my friends. Though there is *always* more to learn, *always* more **ADVENTURES** to go on together, it's never ending really... My hope is that you had a **great** time *trying out* and *trying on* **CARTOON VOICES** and that, **no matter what**, you know that the *joy* of becoming a cartoon character is the *most important* part of all.

In the transformation from real life to the **CARTOON** world, we get to **stretch** to our limits and become our **BIGGEST** selves. The bigger we are, the *more* we feel we can achieve. So I'd like to **congratulate YOU** for taking the **risk** to get here. Oh, and let's thank "**THE GANG**" for showing us **examples** along the way, too.

Till next time,

Sunday Rose

Sunday (the girl who wrote this book, not the day of the week)

P.S. *I have included a few sample audition scripts at* bonus.greatbigvoices.com *for you to practice with.*

P.P.S. *Tell your parents and teachers that I've also created one more section just for them, so they can help you out if need be. I think they'll find it interesting. It's about money, so I bet they'll go for it!*

Okay, bye for now. See you soon, friends!

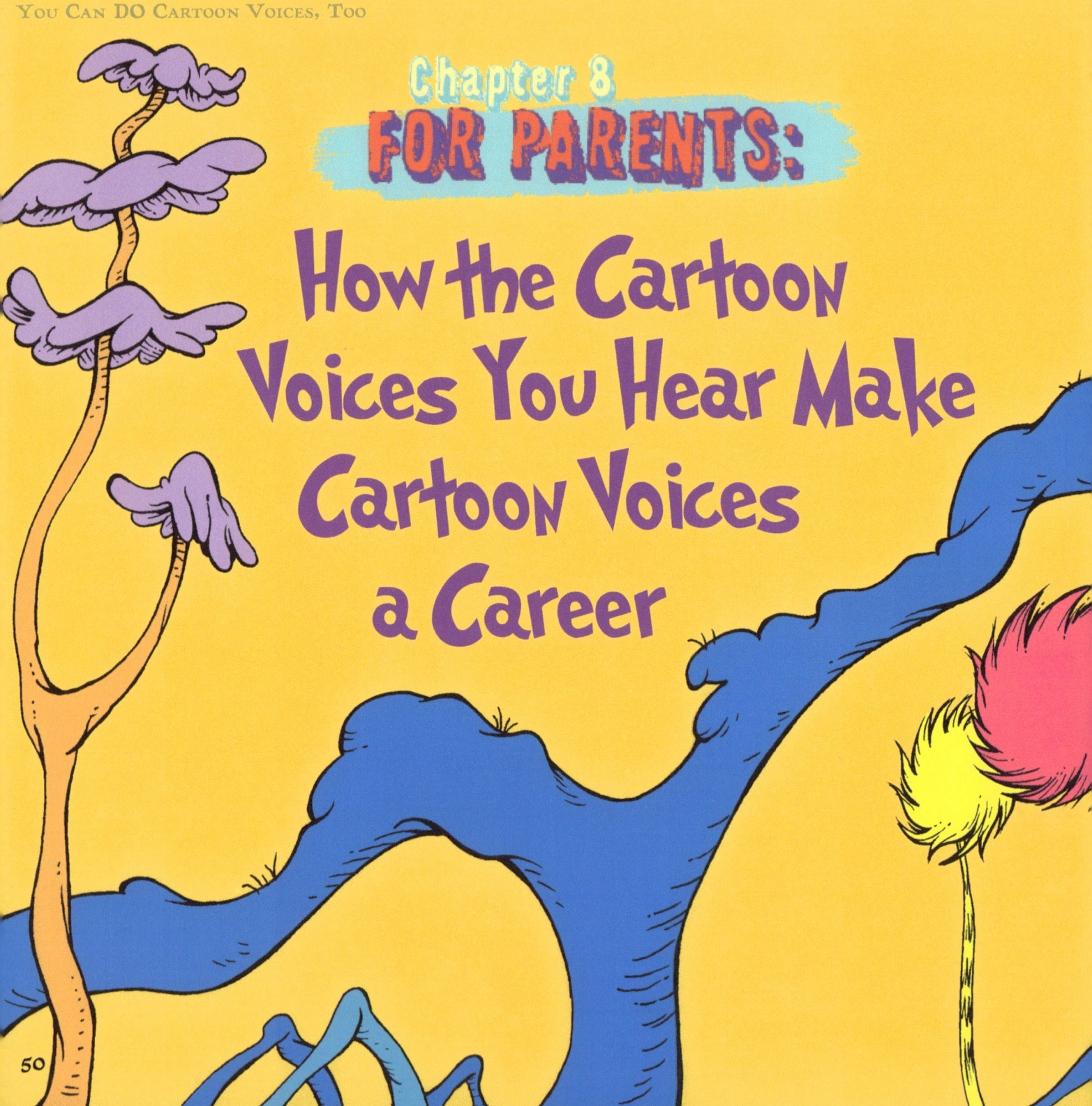

Chapter 8
FOR PARENTS:
How the Cartoon Voices You Hear Make Cartoon Voices a Career

For Parents: Voice Demos

Most agents request a demo so that they can hear your child's voice before meeting you. A voice demo is the equivalent of a head shot for an actor, only it's on a CD. It is something that showcases your child's vocal talents in a really short amount of time. Demos last two minutes maximum. A voice coach organizes your demo and assists in choosing what material to include so that the listener can hear a variety of your child's voices. Some material is improvised or made up, and some may come from actual scripts of shows already airing on TV. It is my experience that kids need some training with voice lessons first, before doing a demo, to fully discover their cartoon voices. For examples of demos, feel free to check out my website at www.sundaymuse.com. All of the talent listed worked very hard before completing his/her demo.

How do cartoons differ from radio commercial voiceovers?

Cartoons require a great deal of energy in the voice, as covered in this book. Unlike our "natural speaking tone," it's important that what is spoken is very projected. Radio commercials are spoken in much the same manner as in "real life talking." The work that needs to be done is in the script breakdown and in making choices. The voice needn't do much other than ' be itself.'

A Peek Behind the Scenes

To give you a realistic look into the life of a child cartoon voice professional, I asked a few top agents in Los Angeles and Canada ten questions I hear a lot from parents who are considering getting their kids into this line of work. Their answers should help you decide whether this is a good idea for your child.

Below are the questions I asked. The agents' answers follow the list.

1) How do you decide whether to take a child on or not?

2) In general, is there work for kids in the voice industry?

3) Can kids earn a good living doing voice work?

4) How should parents approach an agent when seeking representation?

5) How can a child get a meeting with an agent?

6) If a child has already done some voice work but hasn't worked in a while, what would you recommend he/she do?

7) What kinds of things might you suggest a child do in preparation for doing voice-overs? Should they work with a voice coach for cartoons? Have a demo reel?

8) Do you take kids on 'just' for voice-overs? And what does that include? Cartoon as well as commercial voice overs?

9) Is it realistic for a kid to think only of doing voice work for a line of work?

10) Would you recommend a child do some cartoon voice lessons with a coach and build a demo before approaching voice agents?

L.A Agent/CESD Talent Agent Melissa Berger says:

There are many factors that determine if I am going to represent a young actor for voice work. I am always open to good actors with strong resumes. An interesting vocal quality is always a plus. Versatility is important – ability to speak another language fluently or be good with dialects are very attractive attributes. Raspy (textured) voices are very marketable – and as girls get older, they can branch out and do little boy voices – something that is useful in adulthood. There is always a concern when hiring a young teen boy that the project may not be finished before puberty sets in ... I have a number of examples of producers needing to find a "voice match" for someone who has aged out of the role due to the course of nature. In one case, the actor happened to have a younger brother who was able to step in and fill out any rewrites and retakes that were needed once his brother's voice had dropped.

An actor with a strong background in comedy usually does well with voice work; they're used to being fearless and take to the text naturally. By the same token, they have to be grounded and make real choices – organic choices – that come from a place of truth.

There definitely is work for kids in the voice industry! Animated feature films and series cast children and teens all the time. Some are more open to this line of work than others. We all know the Simpsons, King of the Hill and Recess are among those series that use adults to voice children, but Disney, Nickelodeon and Cartoon Network all have series with children and teens playing age-appropriate roles.

Voice work can be very lucrative, but that's always a dangerous reason to pursue it. You have to love the work, because it can take a long time to book something, and if you aren't doing it for passion of the craft, you will not have something to hang onto when your only reward may be the time you have working with the copy and making it your own. And you can work steadily, then suddenly not be booking – perhaps you grow, and you're not fitting a category they're looking for, or you haven't figured out what it takes to move to the next age category. I have had clients who worked constantly from 9 to 11 or 12 years of age, then had a few years where they weren't booking, as they moved beyond the cute natural-sounding child and into the teen category, where they might find themselves competing with adults. Shows change, styles change, and you have to be able to keep up and reinvent.

I prefer to have actors come to me through referrals rather than cold calls – I get a lot of inquiries, like "I'm told my child has a cute voice, and we don't want to have to make the investment an acting career requires, so thought we'd do cartoons ..." Such a misconception! You need to be a stronger actor to book a voice job as a child – you can't just be adorable, you have to be able to act too! I have found that the young actors who start booking voice work quickly almost without exception do well with the on-camera acting part of their career – it can be a good barometer.

A referral from a reputable voiceover teacher or voice director is my preference. I will also take referrals from managers and other agents of actors who have good theatrical training and background, and audition them in our studios to see if they handle copy and would be a good fit for my roster. Even if an actor has a demo, I have them go into the booth to hear what they can do. A demo is nice to have, and I do use them -- we post them on our company website and on an industry-wide website as well -- but most jobs seem to be audition-driven. Occasionally I can use a demo to get a direct offer, but very often, they want to hear the actor with their copy.

I recommend a workshop. If you worked a lot as a 9-year-old child and are now 16, the demands of the roles you are going to play will be different. And your vocal instrument will have changed. Plus a good teacher has their finger on the pulse of the marketplace, so they will be attuned to subtle stylistic changes. Always keep your skills sharp, and keep developing them.

I take young actors on "just for voiceover" but there has to be something special that sets them apart to have me do that. I also have actors theatrically, so to take on a voiceover-only client they need to have a solid theatrical background, interesting voice and preferably some voiceover experience. Accents and fluency in other languages – Spanish being the most requested – are other reasons I would take on a voiceover only actor. When I take on a voiceover client, unless they prefer otherwise, it is for animation (cartoons) as well as commercials.

I have some clients who are amazing voice talents who just have no desire to be in front of the camera. They work a lot, and they balance that with things that are important to them, like school, soccer, whatever. Their parents and the actor may find the voiceover-audition process less intimidating or painful than what on-camera auditions require. Auditions are done on our premises, so they're not driving to be judged by strangers, and the average session is less than four hours. This is a far cry from the hours you spend on a movie set! And it can often be flexible, so you can usually work in those cartoon sessions around your school trip.

I recommend getting training before you approach an agent, even if just to learn booth etiquette. You want to be ready to work with every opportunity that presents itself. You will be much stronger and more confident if you know what you are doing. It takes a while to get there, and if you are serious about your craft it takes an investment … not just money, but time, energy and passion.

Also watch and know the medium. Watch animation, listen to the actors and what they are doing. Learn from them. Listen to the ads on radio and TV when they feature kids just to get a sense of what sort of things are out there. Easiest and most important, read out loud all the time and play with your voice. Don't be afraid to make mistakes. Sometimes the best discoveries come from taking those risks. Have fun!!

Do your best to have your skills be as sharp as possible. Learn accents, play with different characters, understand the genre you are reading for, and when you audition for a preschool show, you will handle that copy differently than if it's a cartoon aimed at older children or a game. Radio spots will require a different style than a preschool show or an animated movie aimed at teens.

*Melissa Berger's clients include series regulars on **Phineas & Ferb**, **Avatar**, **Adventure Time, Bubble Guppies, Ni Hao Kailan, Chowder**, **"Tinkerbell"** in the new **Disney** franchise, plus many more. They have also been heard in loop groups for movies as diverse as **Finding Nemo** and **The Changling**, plus TV series, commercials and radio campaigns.*

Toronto Agent Noelle Jenkinson/AMI says:

There are a number of factors to consider when evaluating a child for voice work. The first and most important is that the child be old enough and have an excellent ability to read. In TV, film and theatre, children memorize their lines. In voice, the scripts are not memorized and are read aloud in the session. Confidence, acting ability and voice quality are also key factors. The child must be able to read cleanly as well as give a great performance.

Desire and commitment to do this type of work are also key. This desire has to be on both the part of the child and the parent(s). The child has to have the desire and the parent has to have the desire to support and commit to this activity for the child. While voice work is a fun activity for a number of kids, it's always good to keep in mind that this is a business and needs the appropriate commitment.

There is a lot of work for kids in the voice industry. The two main areas of work are commercial voice work and Animation.

A really talented child can make a significant amount of money doing voice work. That said, I am always concerned when a parent asks this question. This path should never be chosen as a money making venture for the parent or the child. Because this is a business, and agents make their money strictly on commissions, a good agent will take someone on because they feel that child is marketable as a performer. That said, we need to remember that children need to balance many things. For a child, this industry is work, but it should be enjoyed as much as other activities like dance classes and soccer. The difference is that voice work is an activity for which you get paid.

Talent agencies have different preferences and policies regarding submissions for representation. Phone the agency and ask about the policy for submitting to an agent. My preference is that the parent send me an email regarding their child. In that email I like to hear a voice demo (if the child has one) as well as any experience the child has in acting and/or training in this area.

Next, the parent needs to give the agent some time to review the child's package. Please know that while agents are always interested in new great talent, their first priority is their day-to-day business. That is working for the clients that they already represent. The agent will respond when their schedule allows. It never hurts to follow up with either a phone call or another email if you've heard nothing after a week or so. Leave a clear and detailed message for the agent who will respond when able.

Assuming that the goal is to have the child do more work, the first course of action would be to speak with the child's agent. There could be many factors affecting the child's ability to work. For example:

1. **The age of the child.** Casting specs for children in voice are very narrow (i.e., 10 to 12 years old) as opposed to the casting specs for adults in the industry (i.e., 30 to 40 years old). Sometimes there is a lot of work for kids, but it just may not be in the age range of a particular child.

2. **Voice change.** This is a big factor for boys in the industry. As boys go through voice changes, their work will slow down until their voice settles.

3. **Availability.** Have you been fulfilling your end of this partnership? If your child is frequently not available for auditions and work, you are preventing your agent from being able promote your child.

I think a great place to start is for kids to read their books aloud and give character to each of the various characters in the book they're reading. Training is always a great idea. The children not only learn a new skill set but also learn about the industry as a whole.

Always take lessons from a voice coach who is actively working in the industry. It's great access to first hand experience and knowledge. Demo reels are also helpful. That said, kids' roles in most commercials are not meaty enough to be used on a demo. Creating a demo is great, but not always necessary. Kids' voices change quickly, so a demo can quickly become outdated. Some sort of voice sample is a huge benefit. It allows the agent to submit to casting directors on the odd occasion when an audition is not necessary.

Since AMI is a full-service agency, the majority of the children on the voice roster are already doing on-camera and/or theatre work. I do take children on just for voice. This includes both commercial voice and animation. Parents should keep in mind that these are two different types of voice work requiring different skill sets. Therefore, there is never a guarantee that the child will work in both areas.

It is possible for a child to consider only doing voice. However, having experience in other areas of acting is always an asset and will aid the child in evolving as an actor as they mature.

Noelle Jenkinson's clients include series regulars on Max & Ruby, Arthur, Super Why, Babar, Peep, Busytown, Toot & Puddle, Will & Dewitt, Poppetstown, Willa's Wildlife, Grossology, Pearlie, Save Ums, Atomic Betty, Miss BG, Franklin the Turtle, Miss Spider, Captain Flamingo, Franny's Feet, Wilbur, Calliou, My Friend Rabbit, Jane & The Dragon and many more.

L.A. Agent Cynthia McLean, SBV Talent, says:

Since an agent's relationship with the parent is crucial to the success of my efforts on behalf of the child, I actually make my decisions on two different criteria.

The first criteria are based on the child. The child must be outgoing and friendly and at ease with adults. Since virtually all of the interaction that the child will have in the business will be with adult strangers, they must be comfortable in that setting. Additionally, the child must be interested and enthusiastic about voiceover. If it's the parent's dream and the child would rather be playing outside, it will not work.

The second criteria are based on the parent's expectations. I interview the parents as if they were the one seeking representation. Do they have a reasonable understanding of their child's abilities? Do they have reasonable expectations of what opportunities their child will have? Do they have the time to devote to driving the child to interviews and jobs?

If the above criteria are met, and if I think that the child will thrive in the business and if I think that I could communicate well with the parent, then I would be interested.

There are plenty of opportunities for children in this industry, mostly in animated TV series, and television and radio commercials.

If an appointment is made, the parent should have a clear understanding of the agency and how the relationship with a performer and an agent works, including the commission. I suggest they look at the agency's website and listen to the demos to get an idea of the culture of the agency.

Each agency has its own policy about accepting submissions. Call the receptionist or look at the website to find out if the agency is accepting submissions and how to submit. The best method is through a referral from someone in the industry (i.e., a producer, casting director, acting coach or another performer) who believes in the child.

Cynthia McLean's clients include series regulars on Lilo and Stitch, Chowder, Bubble Guppies, and Higglytown Heroes.

THE END.

*For audio materials and script samples visit: bonus.greatbigvoices.com

ACKNOWLEDGEMENTS

MANY THANKS TO:

Tom Kurzanski, Graham Powell, Keith Eager, John Banks, Andrew Sabiston, Gareth Bennett, Michael Rafelson, THE GANG (Mark, Shemar, Juliana, Liam, Andrea, Zoe) and their wonderful Parents, Nusa from Annex Art Centre, Mike Fallows, Michelle Tocher, John Stevens, Alan Bleviss, Cara Pifko, the staff at Annapurna, Rocco at the Eggplant, Catherine Comuzzi, Mom, Kailey Gilchrist, Joe & Jim Davidson at Clare Burt Studios, Galia Volcovich, Moy and Mery Volcovich, Cecile Just, Lara Lavi from Wide Awake, Sandy McGinty, Todd Dombrowski, Sherry Dayton, Jessie Thomson, Deb Toffan, Noelle Jenkinson, Cynthia McLean, Melissa Berger, Gerald McDermott, Dorothy McCulloch, Bob McCulloch, Gavin McGarry, Leigha Cardella, Jessie Frampton.

and last but not least Charlie & Sally, my Muses.

SUNDAY MUSE

As a leading voice actor and esteemed educator specializing in animation, Sunday's clients have gone on to book roles in major cartoons such as "FAMILY GUY" on FOX, "ARTHUR," "BABAR," "BUSYTOWN," & "SUPER WHY" on PBS (by the creators of "BLUES CLUES"). In addition, top casting directors seek her expertise on casting recommendations for lead roles in animated series sucha as: Disney's "ROLIE POLIE OLIE," "BABAR," "MISS SPIDER," "CARE BEARS" (Playhouse Disney), "FRANKLIN" (ABC kids), "CAILLOU"(PBS), & "ARTHUR" (ABC).

More than a decade ago, Sunday launched "SUNDAY MUSE CARTOON VOICES FOR KIDS & ADULTS" an original workshop as a way of sharing all the valuable tools she gained during her many years as a lead voice for cartoons. Sunday has provided her vocal expertise in such animated hits as Disney's Emmy award winning "ROLIE POLIE OLIE" (Playhouse Disney), "CHEER BEAR/CARE BEARS," "ARTHUR," "JO~JO'S CIRCUS" (Playhouse Disney), Emmy nominated "TIME WARP TRIO" (Discovery Kids NBC), "CAILLOU" (PBS), "WILLA'S WILDLIFE" (Discovery Kids NBC), "ODD JOB JACK" (Comedy Central), "JANE & THE DRAGON" (NBC), "JIMMY 2 SHOES" (Playhouse Disney), and tons more.

As a frequent lecturer, Sunday has taught at NYU, the Children's Theatre Company NYC, Jewish Community Centre NYC, Montessori Schools, Etobicoke School for the Arts, the renowned Koko Productions in Vancouver & the prestigious National Theatre School whose program originates from Michel St.Denis, founding member of Juilliard.

Sunday has also directed a series of animated audio books and has been featured as a guest on various radio shows.

Sunday Muse honed her acting skills on the stages of Second City, National Theatre School, & the Comedy Store.

www.ingramcontent.com/pod-product-compliance
Lightning Source LLC
Chambersburg PA
CBHW042018080426
42735CB00002B/89